THE WORLD TODAY

Terrorism

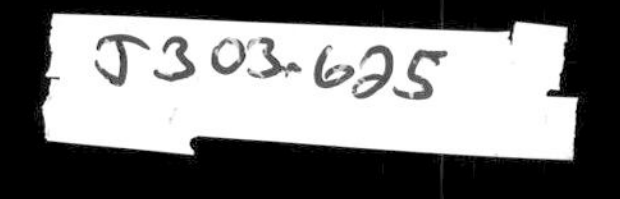

Judith Anderson

First published in 2008
by Franklin Watts

Franklin Watts
338 Euston Road
London NW1 3BH

Franklin Watts Australia
Level 17/207 Kent Street
Sydney, NSW 2000

Editor: Jeremy Smith
Design: Simon Borrough
Art director: Jonathan Hair
Picture Researcher: Diana Morris

Picture credits: AFP/Getty Images: 37. Sabah Arar/Rex Features: 29. Mike Baldwin/Cartoon Stock: 30bl. Dmitry Beliakov/Rex Features: 15. Daniel Berehulak/Getty Images: 39. Photo by the Biblical Archaeology Society of Washington, D.C/Getty Images: 35. Greg Bos/Reuters/Corbis: 32. Pete Canary/Cartoon Stock: 38. CSU Archv/Everett/Rex Features: 14. Beth Dixson/ Alamy: front cover b. © Engelhart/The Hartford Courant: 22. David R. Frazier PhotoLibrary/Alamy: 30r. Hulton Archive/Getty Images: 16t. Marco di Lauro/ Getty Images: 36. Lehtikuva Oy/Rex Features: 6, 16b. Marbella Photo/Rex Features: 9. Alisdair Macdonald/Rex Features: Martin McCullough/Rex Features: 12. Mykel Nicolaou /Rex Features: 31. Courtesy of Plymouth County Jail/Getty Images: 27. Rex Features: 23, 24.Sipa Press/: 13, 18, 19, 20, 21, 26, 28. Ray Tang/Rex Features: 25. TS/Keystone USA/Rex Features: 11. Wilmar Photography/Alamy: 34. Stavchansky Yakov/Shutterstock: front cover t.

Picture research: Diana Morris

A CIP catalogue record for this book
is available from the British Library.

Dewey number: 629.47

ISBN 978 0 7496 8101 2

Printed in China

Franklin Watts is a division of
Hachette Children's Books,
an Hachette Livre UK company
www.hachettelivre.co.uk

Contents

What is terrorism?

Terrorists often try to spread fear among the general public in order to achieve their aims.

Many people think that terrorism is one of the biggest threats in the world today. Yet the risk to most individuals is actually extremely slight. Experts have calculated that while the average US citizen faces a one in 88 chance of dying in a car accident, the risk of dying in a terrorist incident is as little as one in 69,000. But terrorism affects a great many more people than that.

Defining terrorism

Terrorism is generally considered to be a criminal act of violence or destruction that is aimed at members of the public in order to spread fear and disruption, publicise the terrorists' aims and force a government or organisation to act in a certain way. However, the United Nations (UN) has struggled for years to agree on a definition of terrorism that is acceptable to all of its member states. This is because some argue that using violence to bring about change may be acceptable if, for example, people are trying to overthrow an oppressive regime.

laws and governments
police, politicians, media
general public
friends and family
dead and injured

When a terrorist strikes, the effects are felt far beyond the immediate casualties.

Forcing change

Terrorists have a set of aims, or objectives, that they seek to achieve by carrying out acts of violence, or threatening to carry them out. Their aims may be complex, or focused on a single issue such as animal rights or protecting the environment. They often hope to change public opinion by spreading fear and publicising their cause. They may seek to change government policies or they may want to overthrow a government altogether. Terrorists often argue that bringing about change through peaceful means is not possible, and that violence is the only course of action left open to them.

Spreading fear

Not every act of violence is a terrorist act. Terrorism is different from other crimes because it deliberately uses violence to create a sense of fear or panic among the general population. Killing lots of people is not necessarily the main objective. What matters to the terrorist is the knock-on effect. When a bomb goes off, a handful of people may be injured or killed but thousands, even millions, may panic, feel frightened, change their behaviour, ask questions of their government and demand new laws.

THOUGHT BOX

Some people argue that acts of terror are justified in certain circumstances such as the struggle to gain independence from a foreign occupying army or an oppressive government. Do you think there are any circumstances in which violence against civilians is justified?

'When someone uses the **slaughter** of innocent people to advance a so-called political cause, at that point the political cause becomes immoral and unjust.' **Rudolph Giuliani**, Mayor of New York, speaking on the first anniversary of the 9/11 terrorist attacks against the US, 11 September 2002.

In 2004, al-Qaeda bombed several commuter trains in Madrid, killing 191 people and wounding 1,755.

Terrorism in the past

Terrorism is not a new crime. People have used violence to spread fear and crush opposition for thousands of years. The word 'terrorism' was first used to describe the chaos and fear that existed during the French Revolution at the end of the eighteenth century, when thousands of innocent citizens were executed in a period known as 'The Terror'.

The nineteenth century

The nineteenth century was a period of great political and ideological upheaval in Europe. Ethnic groups such as the Serbs in the Balkan region of Europe sought independence from imperial rule in movements that became known as 'nationalist' or 'separatist' struggles. Elsewhere, revolts against aristocratic or oppressive governments developed into 'communist' or 'anarchist' groups, particularly in Russia and central Europe. Bombs were used mainly to highlight a particular cause or to assassinate opponents. Some people argue that these were not true 'terrorist' acts because violence was rarely directed at the general population.

Fenian atrocities

In the nineteenth century, Ireland was ruled by Great Britain. Irish nationalists sought to gain independence from London through a variety of means, some peaceful, some not. The Fenians were a group of Irish nationalists who increasingly used violence and the threat of violence to achieve their aims, culminating in a series of murders and bomb blasts including an attack on the British police headquarters at Scotland Yard in 1884. Members of the public were killed in some of these attacks, and fear was widespread, though this was never the Fenians' main aim.

The Irish Fenians wanted independence and felt unjustly treated by Britain. The Ku Klux Klan wanted to stop non-white, non-protestant Americans from gaining influence in the USA. Both used violence and murder in pursuit of their aims. Do you think one group had more right to carry out terrorist acts than the other?

'A laborer in Cork named Morgan was arrested here to-day on a charge of conspiracy. An important document and a quantity of a compound used in making dynamite were found on his person. Morgan is an employee of a Cork steam-ship company and is accused of... the carrying of arms and explosives between England and this city.' **(From *The New York Times*, April 1883.)**

The Ku Klux Klan

The spread of fear was undoubtedly one of the aims of an organisation known as the Ku Klux Klan (KKK) in the USA in the first half of the twentieth century. The KKK preached racism and anti-Semitism, and sought to intimidate and oppress non-white, non-protestant Americans using violent methods such as arson and murder.

Members of the Ku Klux Klan in the 1920s stand together in full costume around a burning cross.

Changing times

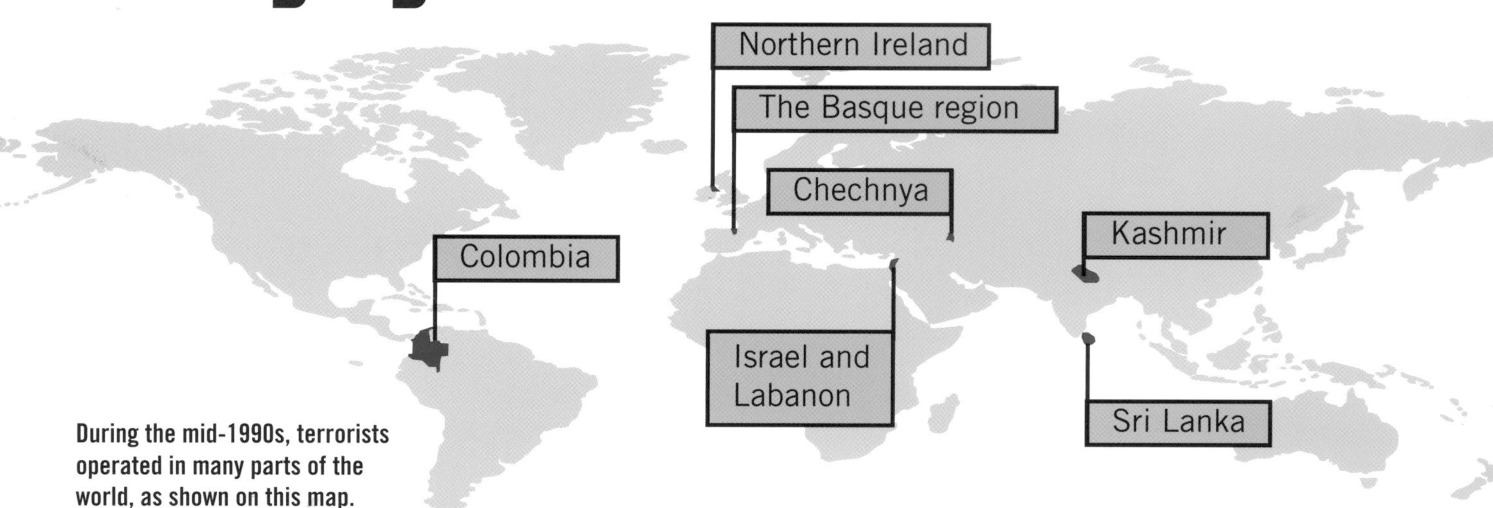

During the mid-1990s, terrorists operated in many parts of the world, as shown on this map.

By the late twentieth century, terrorism had become a familiar tool for some separatist and nationalist groups. From South America to the Russian Caucasus, centuries-old ethnic, religious and political differences were brought into sharp focus. Many terrorists called themselves 'freedom fighters' as they fought to assert their identity on the world stage.

Northern Ireland

The south of Ireland became fully independent from Britain in 1949, but Northern Ireland remained under British rule. Those in Northern Ireland who wanted independence were called Republicans, and those who wanted to remain part of Great Britain were known as Unionists. Both sides included extremists prepared to use bombs and fear to terrorise their opponents and the period from the late 1960s to 1998 became known as The Troubles, when the Irish Republican Army (IRA) and various Unionist paramilitary groups engaged in horrific acts of violence against each other and ordinary people both in Northern Ireland and mainland Britain. In 2005, the IRA abandoned the armed struggle and in 2007, Unionists and Republicans formed a government.

One of the worst atrocities to take place during The Troubles in Northern Ireland was a bomb planted by the 'Real IRA' in Omagh in 1998. It killed 29 innocent people and injured dozens more.

THOUGHT BOX

Journalists and politicians use many different words to refer to those who commit violent acts in the name of independence or revolution. Sometimes they are called terrorists, but they are also called 'paramilitaries', 'freedom fighters', 'guerrillas', 'rebels' and 'soldiers'. What do these different words suggest to you? Does it matter which words we use? Why?

Colombia

Since the 1970s, a group known as Revolutionary Armed Forces of Colombia (FARC) have been waging war against the Colombian government. Their aim is to overthrow the government. Their methods include bombing police stations, assassinating opponents and kidnapping thousands of people every year. They have built up a vast military machine by importing weapons, controlling the export of illegal drugs and forcing children to fight for their cause. The United Nations considers FARC to be a terrorist group.

Sri Lanka

The Liberation Tigers of Tamil Eelam (LTTE) are the military wing of a separatist movement of ethnic Tamil people in Sri Lanka, who seek independence from the ruling Sinhalese government. Sometimes they are referred to as 'rebels' or 'separatist fighters' because they are supported by many ordinary Tamils who view their struggle as 'civil war' rather than terrorism. However, many of their methods – bombs, assassinations, suicide missions – involve terrorising the local population and extorting money in order to fund their campaign.

FARC guerrillas in uniform on the march in Colombia.

'We are not a terrorist organization.'

Daya Master, spokesman for the Liberation Tigers of Tamil Eelam, speaking after the European Union strongly condemned the murder of a Sri Lankan politician in 2005.

A worldwide audience

Terrorists carry out acts of violence for many different reasons. They may want to kill their opponents. They may want to force people to agree to their aims. Sometimes they simply want to draw attention to their cause.

Beyond national borders

Terrorist groups were active in Lebanon, Israel and the Israeli-occupied areas of the Middle East for much of the twentieth century (see pages 16-17). However, the violence rarely spread outside the region and many people in other parts of the world were unaware of what was taking place. This changed in the early 1970s, with a number of high profile hijackings on foreign soil. Then, in 1972, a Palestinian terrorist group known as Black September took Israeli athletes hostage at the Munich Olympics in Germany. In a dramatic gunfight, eleven hostages were killed. Now millions of ordinary people around the world feared that terrorism might come to their country.

Hijackings and hostages

Hijacking a plane and taking innocent people hostage became an alarmingly frequent form of terrorism in the late twentieth century. Part of the reason for this was that governments sometimes felt so pressurised by the threat of mass murder that they gave in to the terrorists' demands, which often involved releasing convicted terrorists from prison or allowing terrorists safe passage to another country.

'At least the world is talking about us now.' **George Habash**, founder of the Popular Front for the Liberation of Palestine, after its 1968 hijack of an Israeli aeroplane.

A hooded terrorist gunman stalks the Munich Olympics in 1972, in scenes that were transmitted live around the world.'

Russian forces stormed the school at Beslan in North Ossetia in an attempt to free the hostages being held by Chechen terrorists.

The impact of television

There is no doubt that television has, at times, helped terrorists to publicise their demands. In September 2004, heavily armed Chechen terrorists held more than 1,200 adults and children hostage in a school in Beslan, in North Ossetia. The terrorists wanted the withdrawal of Russian troops from Chechnya, and chose to target North Ossetians because they were friendly with Russia. They filmed scenes of frightened children next to piles of explosives and the images were broadcast on television, causing terrible anguish to the families of those inside the school. In the end, 334 civilians, including many children, were killed and many hundreds more were injured.

THOUGHT BOX

What terrorists seek is publicity for their cause. They sometimes make films and record messages for television companies to broadcast around the world. Do you think that these films and messages should be banned from television, or do you think that the general public has a right to know what these groups are saying and doing?

This map shows the location of Beslan, in North Ossetia. Terrorists fighting for independence and the withdrawal of troops targetted this area, as it was allied to Russia.

A holy war?

Many people consider the struggle between Palestinians and Jews in the Middle East to be a key factor in understanding terrorism in our world today. If we want to find out about the nature of global terror, we have to look at the origins of the conflict in Israel and the response of the international community to this crisis.

Irgun, a Jewish militant group, bombed the King David Hotel in Israel in 1946, killing 92 people.

The creation of Israel

Since the beginning of the twentieth century, Jewish people began emigrating to what they regarded as their ancient homeland in Palestine and settling alongside the local Muslim population. But tensions soon built up between Jews, who wanted to create a separate Jewish state, and Palestinians, who had inhabited the region for centuries. Fighting broke out and when the Jews declared the creation of the state of Israel in 1948 this developed into full-scale war. Muslim countries such as Syria and Lebanon which bordered Israel were drawn into the conflict too.

Yasser Arafat, leader of the PLO, speaking in 1980: 'Peace for us means the destruction of Israel. We are preparing for an all-out war, a war which will last for generations.'

Decades of violence

After 1948, many Palestinians fled to neighbouring Muslim countries where they lived in refugee camps. Anger at their treatment led to the formation of the Palestinian Liberation Organisation (PLO), with the aim of destroying the new state of Israel. The PLO began to use terror tactics such as hijackings and suicide bomb missions against civilian Jewish targets. Israel tried to strengthen its position with a series of invasions into neighbouring territories, and the crisis deepened. Since the 1990s, the international community has been negotiating for the creation of a separate Palestinian state, but this has not yet been established and the hatred and fear on both sides means that violence is still never far away.

Religion and terror

The conflict in the Middle East has always been about more than land. Jerusalem, an ancient city inside Israel, is a place of huge religious significance for Muslims, Jews and Christians alike. Any attack on a holy site is seen as an attack against a particular religion. This inspires religious extremists on all sides to call the conflict a 'holy war', in the name of which they may carry out suicide bombings and the targeting of civilians. Leaders of all three religions specifically denounce such acts but this does not stop extremists, sometimes known as fundamentalists, from using religion to justify their methods.

THOUGHT BOX

The Palestinian cause has inspired many different Islamic or jihadi terrorist groups across the region, including Hezbollah in Lebanon, Hamas in the Palestinian territories and Islamic Jihad in Egypt and elsewhere. All have conducted horrifying attacks on civilians, and list the destruction of Israel amongst their aims. Now ordinary Palestinians have voted for Hamas members to be their leaders. Do you think Israel should try to work with Hamas to bring peace to the region?

Israel is a tiny country (shown right in detail and on a world map below), but it has been supported by many 'western' states including the United States. The Palestinians have been supported by neighbouring Muslim countries.

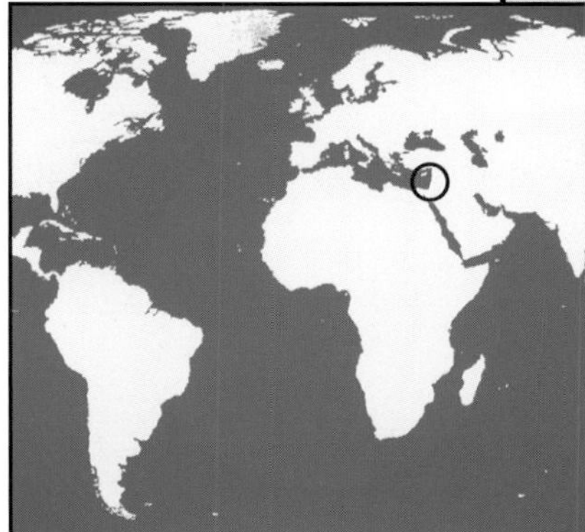

Jihad

In the 1990s, a new type of terrorist appeared. Small groups of Islamic extremists across the Middle East began to talk about a holy war, or jihad, against the United States and its allies. To them, the United States symbolised all that was corrupt and anti-Islamic in the world, but they also showed contempt for any country which they felt did not sufficiently resist western domination. These jihadis were not interested in negotiation – only elimination.

THOUGHT BOX

Osama bin Laden tops the list of dangerous men and women most wanted by the United States. Do you think that capturing Osama bin Laden and other jihadi leaders would help or hinder the fight against global terror?

Al-Qaeda

In 1988, a well-educated Saudi called Osama bin Laden established a small group of extremists most often known as al-Qaeda. Many of al-Qaeda's members first trained in camps in Afghanistan, Sudan and Lebanon. In the 1990s, they began to attack targets all over the world, including US embassies in Africa and US soldiers and civilians in the Middle East. However, while Osama bin Laden may have masterminded many of al-Qaeda's public statements, there appears to be no single organisational structure for the many groups that form the al-Qaeda network. Attacks could come from anywhere at any time.

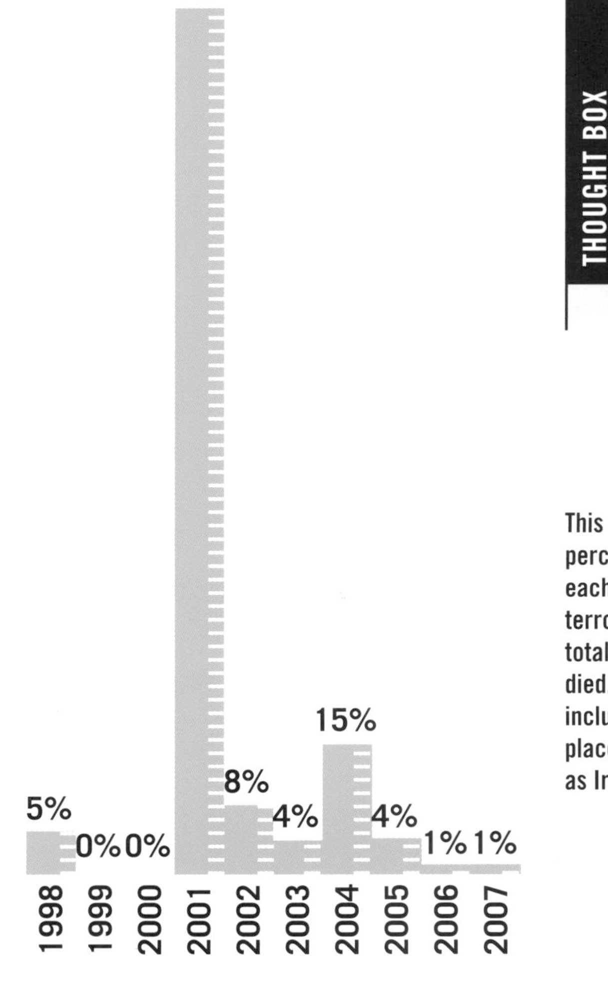

This chart shows the percentage of people killed each year in major al-Qaeda terrorist attacks in which a total of 4,881 people have died. The attacks do not include those that have taken place in countries at war, such as Iraq and Afghanistan.

'Al-Qaeda is a cloak patched together from different sources of discontent... Bin Laden's skill is to transform particular grievances into a universal struggle.'

Rachid, a young Algerian who has been jailed for his association with terrorists. (From ***The Observer***, 9 March 2003)

New recruits

Al-Qaeda recruits come from all parts of the Muslim world. Some originally fought against the Russian occupation of Afghanistan in the 1980s, but new members have emerged in countries such as Pakistan, where a lack of state schools means that young boys can be taught extremist beliefs, without any outside interference. Others, including some European-born Muslims, have turned to terrorism as a way to oppose the USA's military presence in the Middle East, Iraq and elsewhere. All appear united by a fanatical interpretation of Islam.

Moderate Muslims

Most Muslims around the world are horrified by the new, global threat from groups such as al-Qaeda. But those who believe that the Muslim faith teaches peace and non-violence sometimes find that they are targets. Osama bin Laden and other jihadis have demanded the deaths of any Muslims who appear to negotiate with the United States and its allies, and in 2007, they issued a fatwa (judgment) against the Muslim president of Pakistan, Pervez Musharraf, for his attempts to crack down on Islamic terrorism.

The al-Qaeda attack on the US embassy in Nairobi in 1998 killed 12 Americans and 201 others, almost all Kenyans. About 5,000 people were injured.

New Yorkers watch the horror unfold on 11 September, 2001.

On 11 September 2001, a group of al-Qaeda terrorists hijacked four American planes and flew two of them into the Twin Towers in New York. Another was flown into the US defence headquarters known as The Pentagon, while the fourth plane crashed into a field before it reached its target in Washington DC. Nearly 3,000 innocent people died that day.

Terror on US soil

The death and destruction caused by the attacks, the media coverage they received and the shock and fear that followed were unprecedented. Up until then, few people in the USA had considered the possibility that they might be victims of terrorism. Now, everyone felt vulnerable. People looked to their leaders to protect them. The US government had to act.

A shocked world

It wasn't just people in the United States who were shocked and horrified by the events that became known as 9/11. Many countries lost citizens in the attacks on the Twin Towers, and the world knew that al-Qaeda's threats extended to all allies of the US. 9/11 was not the first terror attack, nor the last, but to many it felt like the most shocking event, striking at the heart of New York's business district and demonstrating that al-Qaeda would stop at nothing in pursuit of its goals.

More attacks

Sure enough, more attacks against US allies followed. Bombs in a resort in Bali in 2002 appeared to have been aimed at Australian tourists and 202 people were killed. Spain was attacked in 2004, when bombs on trains in Madrid killed 191 people. The UK's turn came in 2005, when British-born terrorists exploded bombs on public transport, killing 52 civilians. That same year, 89 were killed in bomb attacks in an Egyptian resort.

'Today, our fellow citizens, our way of life, our very freedom, came under attack in a series of deliberate and deadly terrorist attacks.'
George W Bush, US President, 11 September 2001.

THOUGHT BOX

What do you think the terrorists hoped to gain by hijacking planes and attacking the Twin Towers and The Pentagon? Do you think they achieved their aims?

In a poll conducted in September 2007, six years after 9/11, 81 per cent of Americans said the terrorist attacks that day were 'the most significant historical event of their lives'.
(Poll: Zogby International)

Afghanistan

After 9/11, the US government quickly identified al-Qaeda as their main suspects and began to plan a counter-attack in an attempt to root out Osama bin Laden and other jihadi leaders. The focus for this counter-attack was Afghanistan, where many terrorists were believed to be hiding. This was the start of a campaign that became known as the 'War on Terror'.

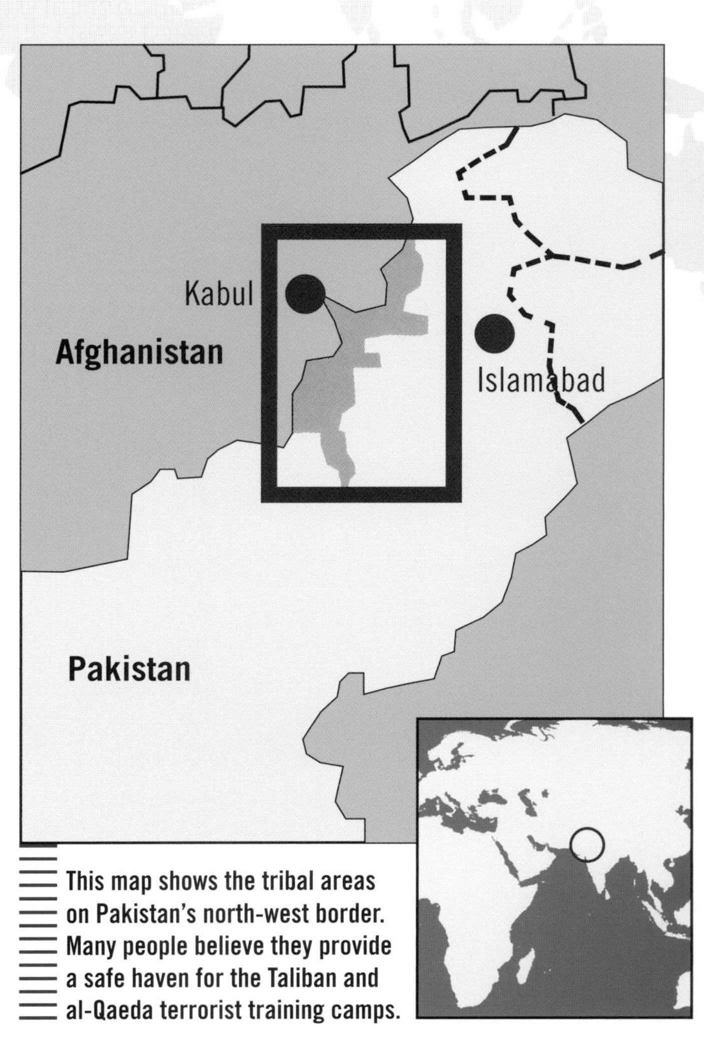

This map shows the tribal areas on Pakistan's north-west border. Many people believe they provide a safe haven for the Taliban and al-Qaeda terrorist training camps.

The Taliban

By the mid-1990s, Afghanistan was a war-torn country ravaged by years of Russian invasion and counter-attack by tribal Afghan fighters. A group of highly disciplined Islamic extremists known as the Taliban emerged in power, conquering the capital, Kabul, in 1996 and imposing a strict, fundamentalist regime on the country.

This cartoon shows US president George W Bush leaving no stone unturned in the hunt for Osama bin laden.

'If inciting people to do that [the 9/11 attacks] is terrorism, and if killing those who kill our sons is terrorism, then **let history be witness** that we are terrorists.' **Osama bin Laden**, speaking in October 2001.

The terror connection

Osama bin Laden fought against the Russians in Afghanistan in the early 1990s. He forged strong links with the Taliban, who, like him, detested liberal Western freedoms and values. Many al-Qaeda members were recruited from the ranks of the Taliban, and training camps were established in the remote, Taliban-controlled mountainous border area between Afghanistan and its neighbour, the Islamic country Pakistan.

A war on terror

The US government took swift action after 9/11. With its coalition allies (including the UK and some anti-Taliban Afghan fighters) it invaded Afghanistan in October 2001 with the intention of destroying al-Qaeda forces and getting rid of the Taliban. The Taliban government was swiftly defeated and a new government installed, but Osama bin Laden was not captured, and Taliban insurgents retreated to their bases in the mountains. They continue to fight US-led coalition forces.

US president George W Bush speaks beside the newly elected president of Afghanistan, Hamid Karzai. June 2002.

THOUGHT BOX

In December 2007, Hamid Karzai, president of Afghanistan, said 'Afghanistan is not a hideout for terrorism, it is a victim of terrorism'. What do you think he meant?

Counter-terrorism

Al-Qaeda and other terrorist organisations had been carrying out attacks against civilians long before the events of 9/11. However, the attacks against the United States in 2001 united many countries around the world who now feared attacks on their own citizens. Some supported the invasion of Afghanistan, but governments also looked for other ways to try to catch terrorists and prevent future attacks.

This CCTV image shows the men who carried out the bombings in London in July 2005. It helped police to trace their movements but it did not stop the attacks from taking place.

'We will only seek new powers that are essential to the fight against terrorism.' **Gordon Brown**, UK prime minister, speaking in 2007.

Greater surveillance

In October 2001, the Patriot Act became law in the United States. The Patriot Act contained many new powers for law enforcement agencies, including the power to detain and deport anyone suspected of terrorist activity and the power to search telephone and email communications. This was felt to be particularly important in the light of the fact that the 9/11 attackers had come to the United States several months before and had even learned to pilot planes at US flight schools. Other countries such as the UK and Australia, soon enacted similar laws.

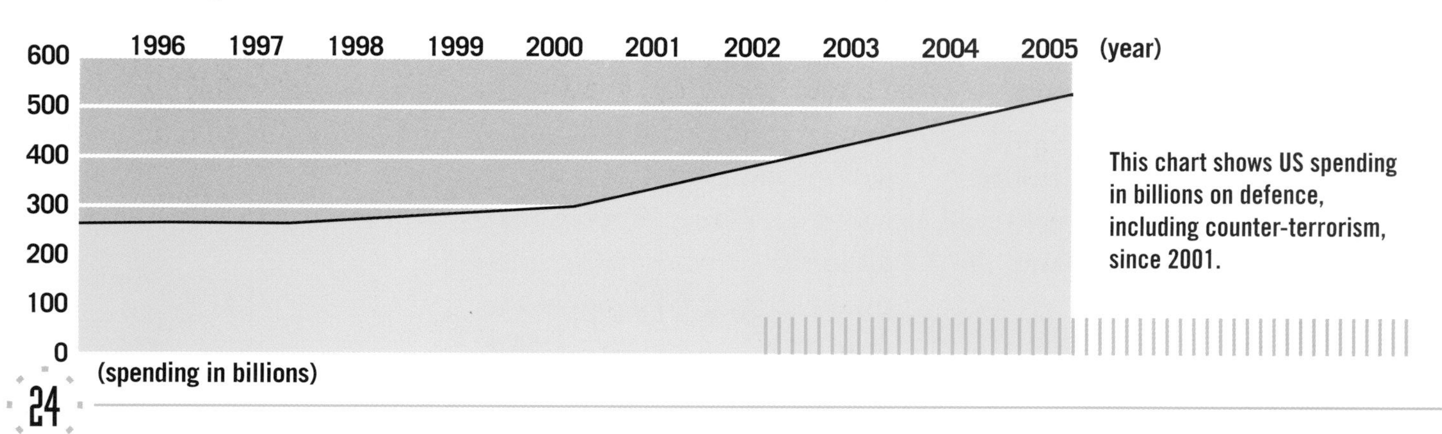

This chart shows US spending in billions on defence, including counter-terrorism, since 2001.

Passengers at airports now face increased security measures such as hand-baggage checks.

New restrictions

Many countries have introduced tighter border controls, with extra screening of airline passengers and their baggage. The UK has established a Border Agency to monitor those coming in and out of the country more closely and has developed new biometric visas and passports that are designed to make it more difficult to forge such documents.

International cooperation

Some countries have signed agreements aimed at pursuing terrorists across national borders and sharing information about terrorist activity. Members of the European Union, have adopted the EU Counter-Terrorism Strategy, which covers four key strands: 'Prevention, Protection, Pursuit and Response'. Prevention means preventing people from turning to terrorism in the first place. Protection means improved security against attack. Pursuit means investigating terrorists across borders, bringing them to justice and cutting off their support and funding networks. Response involves making appropriate preparations for dealing with a terrorist attack.

THOUGHT BOX

It is virtually impossible to assess the effectiveness of counter-terrorism measures, because only those attacks that succeed offer hard statistical evidence. However, the US defence budget indicates the huge cost of such measures. Do you think that this money should be focused on any particular aspect of Prevention, Protection, Pursuit and Response? Or are all four strands equally important?

Dealing with suspected terrorists

Many of the new anti-terror laws have raised important issues for those concerned with human rights and freedoms. Some of the fiercest debate has focused on the way that governments deal with those they suspect of any kind of terrorist activity.

Guantanamo Bay

After the invasion of Afghanistan in 2001, the USA had to decide what to do with the suspected al-Qaeda militants it had captured there. Hundreds were sent to a US naval base at Guantanamo Bay in the Caribbean, where they were declared 'illegal combatants' rather than prisoners of war by the US government. But during the months and years that followed, many observers argued that their incarceration without trial, without a fair hearing and without access to lawyers and their families was inhumane and unjust. Others argue that these prisoners are so dangerous to national security that they cannot be released.

THOUGHT BOX

The United Nations has condemned the use of torture under any circumstances. However, sometimes the USA sends terror suspects overseas to countries where torture is known to have taken place. Do you think there are any circumstances under which torture is acceptable – in order to gain information about a major terrorist attack, for example?

Prisoners suspected of involvement in terrorism are held at Guantanamo Bay.

Detention without charge

In the period after 9/11, many countries had to decide how to deal with people they suspected of involvement with terrorism. The traditional view of a suspect being innocent until proven guilty had to be balanced with the need to protect the public from any potential threat. In the UK, attempts were made to hold terrorist suspects for up to 90 days without the need to charge them with any criminal offence, in order for the police to gather all the necessary evidence. This was reduced to 28 days but some people, including the police, argue that suspects should be held for as long as necessary.

Racial profiling

Another controversial aspect of new counter-terrorism measures is the way that people are assessed to see whether or not they might present a terrorist threat. Al-Qaeda terrorists are associated with Islam, and *may* be of Arabic or Middle Eastern appearance. Yet many argue that if security personnel and the police pay particular attention to one group of people then they are guilty of racism and prejudice against innocent, peaceful Muslims.

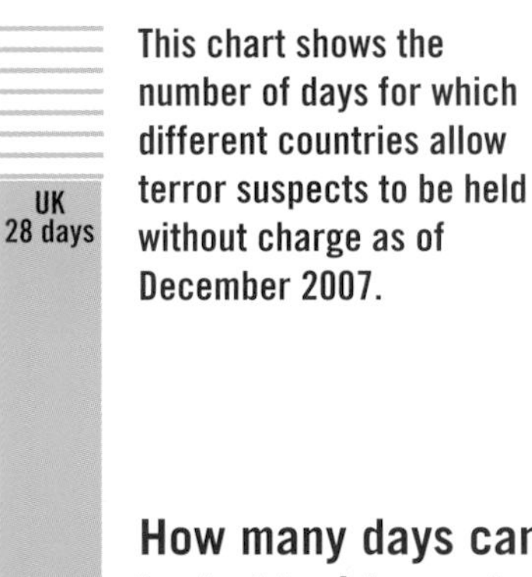
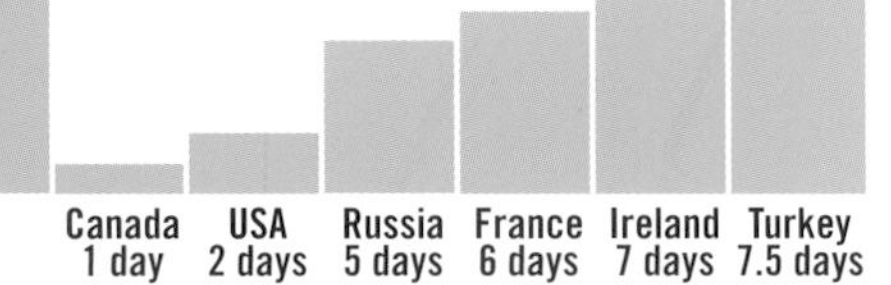

How many days can you be held without charge?

This chart shows the number of days for which different countries allow terror suspects to be held without charge as of December 2007.

Richard Reid (right) admitted trying to blow up a plane using bombs hidden in his shoes. He was born in London of a white mother and a Jamaican father.

'It's OK, you can pass. You don't look like a terrorist!' Spoken by a police officer to a young woman the day before an IRA bomb exploded in a hotel in Brighton in 1984.

Iraq

In March 2003, a US-led multinational force invaded Iraq. The reason given for the invasion was to protect the USA and its allies from the weapons of mass destruction that they argued were being developed within the country. But no such weapons were found and the occupying force soon discovered that peace would not be established quickly or easily.

Aftermath of invasion

It didn't take long for the coalition forces to defeat Iraq's leader, Saddam Hussein. But, rather than a new era of democracy and peace for the country, what followed was a growing insurgency against the invaders and a bitter struggle between different factions and ethnic groups within Iraq. The country was sliding towards civil war.

American soliders inspect the aftermath of a recent suicide bombing attack in Basra, Iraq.

A US poll in June 2007 asked people whether the invasion of Iraq made them feel more or less safe from terrorist attacks in the future.

'You're certainly **not** going to hear from me that al-Qaeda is **defeated** and that **victory** is at hand.' **Ryan Crocker**, US Ambassador in Iraq.

Links to al-Qaeda

In August 2003, a suicide bomber demolished the UN's offices in Baghdad, the capital of Iraq. At least 20 people were killed. In the months and years that followed, Iraqi politicians and religious leaders, police and international non-governmental agencies such as the Red Cross were frequently targeted by rival factions. Officials began to blame some of the attacks on those with links to al-Qaeda and jihadis claimed they were avenging the abuse of Iraqi prisoners held by the USA.

A new generation of terrorists?

Whether or not the new Iraqi government manages to assert its control over the country, what is clear is that the invasion of Iraq has prompted a deadly civil war and provided an excuse for a new wave of terrorists to seek revenge against those who support the US-led coalition forces. The jihadis don't want peace in Iraq. They want the violence and chaos to continue so that anti-American feeling remains high.

THOUGHT BOX

When President Bush declared 'we are fighting the enemy in Iraq and Afghanistan and across the world so we do not have to face them here at home', most counter-terrorism officials around the world disagreed. Many stopped talking about 'the war on terror' after the invasion of Iraq. Why do you think this was?

A different world

In the first decade of the twenty-first century, terrorism has become a global threat and governments spend billions on security and defence. No country seems safe. But how has the world changed for ordinary people?

Travel

Only in the immediate aftermath of 9/11 did the number of people taking flights dip slightly. Flying continues to be one of the statistically safest methods of travel, but more people now experience the increased security measures at airports, railway stations and in other public places, and polls indicate that most travellers are prepared to tolerate the inconvenience this can cause.

This cartoon shows a man being screened before getting into a taxi.

'Fanaticism has always existed. The terrifying thing now is that the **weapons available to the fanatics** are both more lethal and more easily delivered, and that's what makes terrorism, modern terrorism, so much more threatening.'
John Howard, former Australian prime minister, speaking in July, 2005.

Fear

A significant shift has taken place in opinions about the risk of terrorism. When a plot to blow up transatlantic planes was discovered and stopped in the UK in 2006, polls showed an increase in fears about a terrorist attack rather than a decrease due to the effectiveness of counter-terrorism measures. Fear may not stop people from travelling, but it publicises the terrorists' cause and makes people want change.

Tolerance

Are people any more suspicious now of strangers, of people from different cultures or religious beliefs? Because groups like al-Qaeda identify themselves with Islam, are peaceful Muslims a target for suspicion and intolerance? Around the world, many Muslim groups have felt it necessary to issue statements condemning terrorism in all its forms. Creating intolerance is a stated aim of al-Qaeda.

Governments and individuals must work hard to ensure that this is not achieved.

THOUGHT BOX

US President George W. Bush said 'There will be no going back to the era before September 11th, 2001, to false comfort in a dangerous world.' Do you agree?

Sir Iqbal Sacranie, head of the Muslim Council of Great Britain, which states that 'Averting a terrorist attack is an Islamic imperative.'

State-supported terror

In 1988, a passenger plane was blown up over Lockerbie in Scotland, killing 270 people. Many people believed that the Libyan government had ordered the bombing. The UN imposed heavy sanctions against Libya which were not lifted until Libya said it accepted 'responsibility for the actions of its officials' and agreed to pay compensation to the victims' families.

Not all terrorists work against the state. Governments may provide support to a particular group, and sometimes governments carry out their own acts of terror, often to assert their authority or crush opposition. This may be through official channels such as the police, or through more hidden means such as turning a blind eye to thugs and vigilantes.

'There are many **unanswered questions** about who ordered this vile act and why our relatives were not protected.' **Jim Swire**, father of one of the victims of the Lockerbie crash.

State-sponsored terror

Many terrorist groups do not operate alone. They need money, and a safe haven, and sometimes this is provided by a state that supports their cause. Iran admits to sponsoring groups such as Hezbollah in Lebanon and various factions in Iraq, but it denies that these are terrorist organisations. Nevertheless, the USA has placed Iran at the top of its list of states that sponsor terror.

Crushing opposition

Terrorists aren't always extremists. Nor are they always fighting for a cause. Sometimes an act of terror is carried out by a government or an organisation simply so that it can maintain, or increase, its power. In Zimbabwe, President Mugabe's Zanu-PF party has been involved in the deliberate destruction of homes and other acts of violent intimidation in order to crush any opposition to Mugabe's regime.

Manipulating public opinion

Sometimes governments manipulate public opinion through the use of terror. When bombs exploded in several Moscow apartment buildings in 1999, the Russian government was quick to blame Chechen terrorists. However, Russian security services were discovered planting a bomb in an apartment block themselves (though they later claimed this was for training purposes). Many outside Russia suspected the Russian government of secretly using bombs against its own people in order to stir up anti-Chechen feeling. However, this has never been proved.

THOUGHT BOX

In 1985, agents of the French intelligence services deliberately sank the Rainbow Warrior, a Greenpeace ship, to prevent her from interfering in a nuclear test off the coast of New Zealand. Was this an act of state-supported terror? Two agents were caught, but they were convicted of arson and murder rather than terrorism.

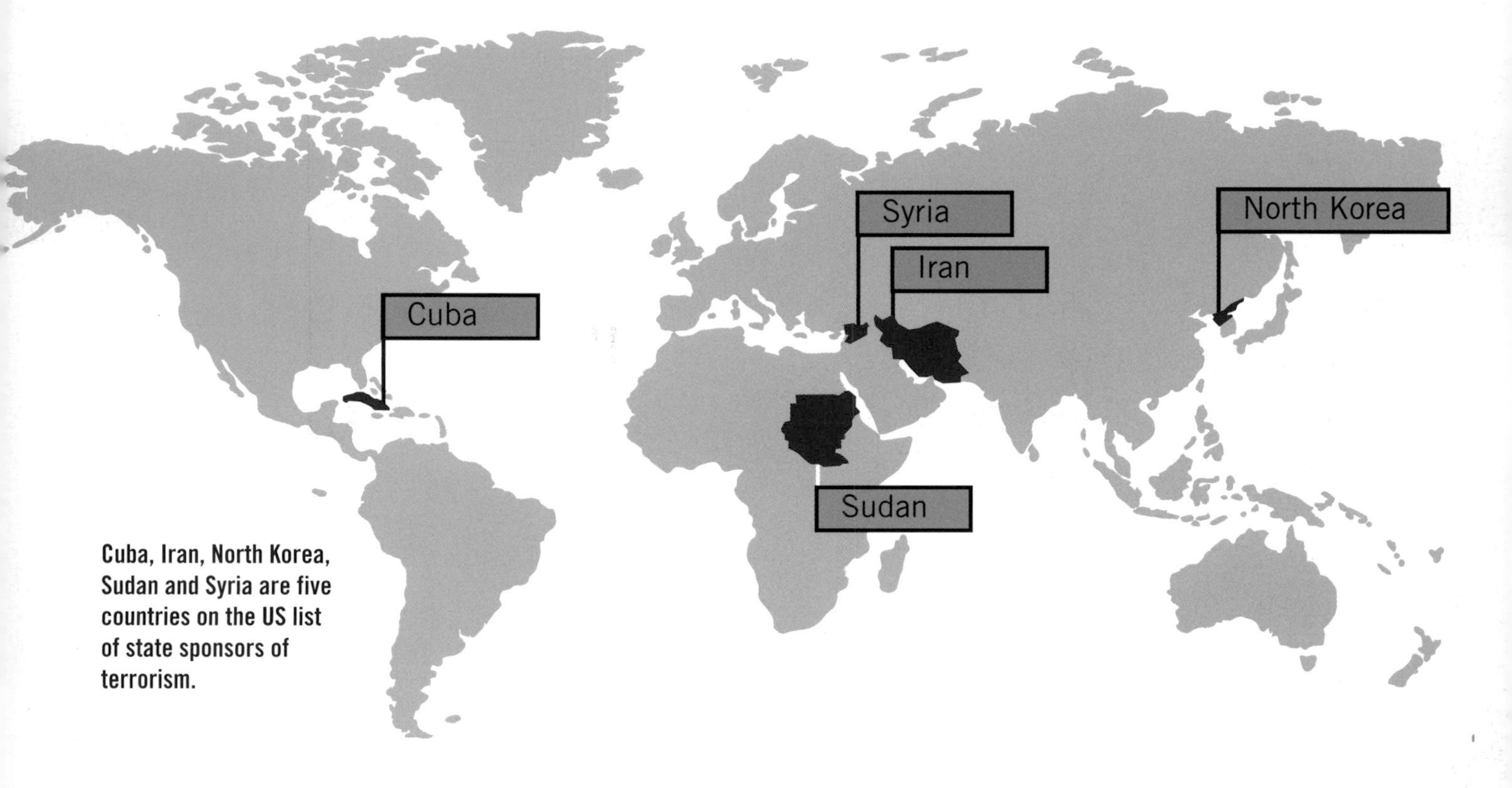

Cuba, Iran, North Korea, Sudan and Syria are five countries on the US list of state sponsors of terrorism.

Funding terror

Terrorism is an expensive affair. Obtaining weapons and explosives, training men, moving them around, providing vehicles and safehouses – all of these things cost money. Sometimes this comes directly from states that sponsor terror, but often it has to come from sources that are more secretive and difficult to trace.

An international trail

A great deal of the money for international terrorists such as al-Qaeda comes from the Middle East, while others raise funds from ethnic expatriates living overseas. But first the money has to be 'laundered' so that it cannot easily be traced. It might pass through private banks, or be broken down into untraceable small amounts, or disguised as charitable donations or transferred through personal contact that avoids paper or electronic evidence.

'Iran has been the country that has been in many ways a kind of **central banker for terrorism.'**

Condoleezza Rice, US Secretary of State, March 2006.

Countries such as Iran (below) are considered by some people as state sponsers of terrorism.

THOUGHT BOX

Terrorist groups need money, but it doesn't actually take much for a single suicide bomber to make a bomb and detonate it in a public place. So why is 'following the money' seen as so important by those working in counter-terrorism?

Faked Middle Eastern artefacts, such as this Sumerian sarcophagos, being shipped around the world to raise funds for terrorism, according to the UK's Metropolitan Police.

Profits of crime

Much of the funding for terrorism is believed to come from the profits of illegal activities such as drug smuggling and arms dealing. Precious gems, such as diamonds that are mined in African war zones, also find their way into illegal channels, heading for the Middle East. The Tamil Tigers are suspected of extorting funds from the expatriate Tamil community in Canada, while a few groups such as the FARC in Colombia rely heavily on kidnapping and the payment of ransom money (see page 13).

Following the money

Individual governments and the UN's Counter-Terrorism Task Force know that one way to intercept terrorists is to follow the money trail from its source to its destination. This requires extensive cooperation between the security services, customs officials and banks of different countries, but such cooperation is not always forthcoming between those that are traditionally hostile towards each other, such as Pakistan and India.

Estimated cost of mounting a terrorist attack:

9/11 attacks in the USA in 2001, killing over 2,800 people: $250,000

Bali nightclub bombings in 2002, killing 202 people: $15,025

Jakarta hotel bombing in 2003, killing 13 people: $15,025

Cyber-terrorism

Cyber-terrorism is a term often used to describe the act of gaining unauthorised access to a computer system or using the Internet to cause severe disruption to real-world services such as airports and power plants. However, some people argue that this is not really terrorism, as it doesn't use physical violence.

How real is the threat?

The internet is a complex web of electronic information, with few restrictions. As such, it has become an active postbox for terrorists, who are able to share information, propaganda and expertise across anonymous websites. Yet while many fear that a terrorist *might* be able to carry out an attack on a country's military systems or infrastructure via a computer, some analysts argue that it is still much easier, and more damaging, for a terrorist to visit a target in person and plant a bomb.

Banking and finance

Nevertheless, the banking and finance sector may be at particular risk from this kind of electronic terrorism. Bombing a bank might kill people, but it would not disrupt an entire country's economy or cause widespread panic in the financial markets in the way that a successful cyber-attack might. And causing widespread panic and disruption is a key aim for many terrorist groups.

How might an act of cyber-terrorism affect you?

When this Russian war memorial was dismantled in Estonia in 2007, objectors responded with a wave of cyber-attacks.

> 'There's been a lot of hype about cyber-terrorism but we have to look at how society has changed. **Young terrorists have grown up with computers.'**
>
> **Rob Martin**, manager of digital services for British Petroleum.

According to NATO (the North Atlantic Treaty Organization) there are five reasons why cyber-terrorism is a possible option for terrorists:

- It is **less expensive** than traditional methods.
- It is **more anonymous** and difficult to trace.
- The **target base** is much larger.
- Attacks can be carried out **remotely**.
- It can affect **larger numbers** of people than traditional methods.

The hackers who gained access to the Estonian computer systems in 2007 appear to have been politically motivated, and intent on causing maximum disruption. But were they terrorists?

The case of Estonia

In May 2007, Estonia came under attack from computer hackers who caused the websites of many government departments, banks and businesses to temporarily shut down. Many of these attacks were made from addresses within Russia and appeared to be a result of anger about the removal of a Russian war memorial from a street in Estonia's capital city. The defence ministry compared the attacks to 'terrorist activities', but others believed that they were simply the work of a number of individuals who chose to express their opinions in this way.

From terrorist to leader

Sometimes, people who have previously been associated with terrorist activities, but who believed they were fighting to liberate people from an oppressive regime, become accepted and recognised as leaders. Members of Sinn Fein in Ireland, the Palestine Liberation Organisation in the Middle East and the African National Congress in South Africa have renounced terrorism and become part of mainstream politics in their respective countries.

'Arafat dies.' Yasser Arafat was leader of the Palestinian Liberation Organisation. Although he renounced violence in his later years and even shared the Nobel Peace Prize with two Israeli leaders, this cartoon marks his death in 2004 by recalling his terrorist past.

Changing times

In the second half of the twentieth century, the white South African government imposed a system known as apartheid, segregating black people and denying their basic rights. The African National Congress (ANC) opposed apartheid and used its military wing, known as Umkhonto we Sizwe (MK), to carry out acts of sabotage and violence in protest against what was happening in the country. The ANC activist and MK commander, Nelson Mandela, was jailed for many years from where he worked tirelessly to promote ideas of freedom and equality. Eventually the government had to accept that apartheid could not continue and Mandela was released. He was awarded the Nobel Peace Prize in 1993 and in 1994 was elected president of South Africa.

THOUGHT BOX

Should a terrorist who renounces violence and works instead for peace still be made to pay for his or her past crimes?

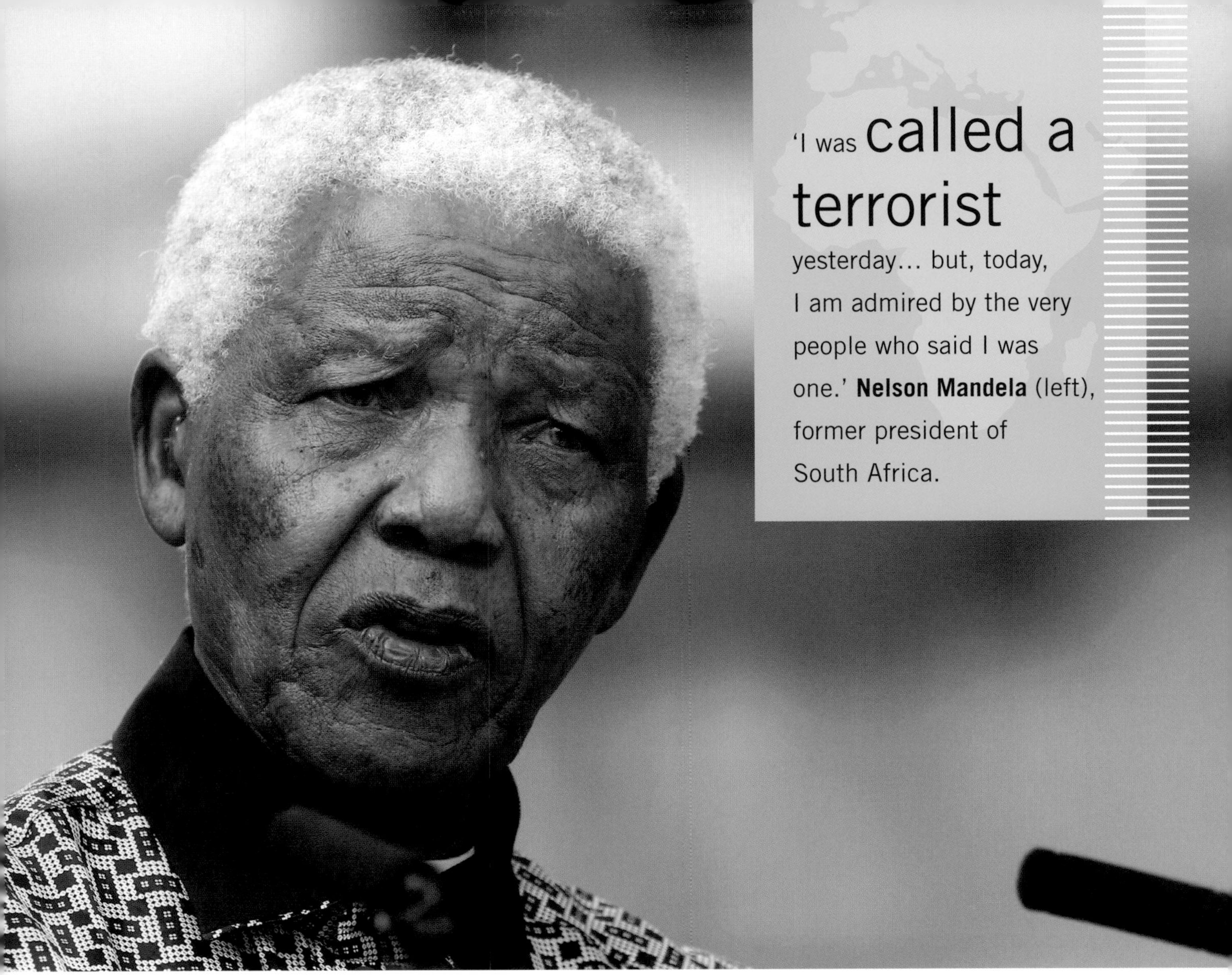

'I was called a terrorist yesterday... but, today, I am admired by the very people who said I was one.' **Nelson Mandela** (left), former president of South Africa.

The failure of terrorism

Sometimes the tide of public opinion turns against terrorist organisations because people become sickened and disillusioned with the violence. The IRA had conducted a campaign of bombings and intimidation for many years in Northern Ireland in an attempt to achieve independence from the UK, but in the end even those who had been sympathetic to its aims could see that its methods were not working. In 2005, the IRA renounced violence and Martin McGuinness, once an IRA commander, was elected Deputy First Minister of Northern Ireland in 2007.

A desire for peace

There continues to be a marked difference between those terrorist groups for whom a political settlement is a goal, and those groups who refuse to acknowledge the value of negotiation and peace. In the Middle East, some Palestinian groups are willing to negotiate with Israel, and recognise that peace between Palestinians and Israelis is essential for the future of both sides. But the charter of the more militant Palestinian Hamas organisation still aspires to the elimination of Israel, so direct negotiation between Hamas and Israel remains unlikely and the violence continues.

Into the future

Terrorists: 21%

United States and allies: 32%

Unsure: 1%

Neither side: 46%

This US poll from December 2007 asked members of the public who they thought was winning the 'war on terror'.

In recent years, the idea of 'global terrorism' (in contrast to local or national terrorist groups) has imposed itself on our lives and in our minds. As technology becomes more sophisticated and communications become more advanced, terror networks such as Al-Qaeda appear to be able to export their violence all over the world. But future terrorist activity will depend to a large extent on how the general public respond.

A different kind of war

Nowadays, the notion of a 'war on terror', in which terrorists are somehow defeated by military force, has become less fashionable amongst the media and politicians. Increasingly, counter-terrorism involves looking at why people become terrorists in the first place, and seeking to prevent the circumstances under which this might occur. The fight is about ideas as much as weapons.

THOUGHT BOX

Terrorists want to change the way people think, vote or behave. Governments have a duty to protect their citizens, and often respond to bombs and threats with tighter security and military force. Others believe we should respond by continuing to exercise our democratic freedom, doing what we want and showing tolerance, not fear. What do you think?

The best way to beat the terrorists is to carry on our everyday lives as normal, and not to become fearful of people who look different from ourselves.

'The best way to defeat the terrorists is to go back to work on the Tube, to dress and work how I want as a woman, to have no fear of other cultures or creeds.' **Rachel North**, injured in the London terrorist bombings of July 2005.

New enemies

New types of terror and terrorist causes are likely to occur in the future. Already, militant groups of animal rights and environmental activists cause more damage to property and issue more threats against individuals in the United States than all the other types of terrorism put together. Religious cults surface from time to time, and sometimes they use violence in pursuit of their cause. Weapons may change too. Nuclear, biological and chemical weapons are all capable of causing terrible destruction and widespread panic.

Here to stay?

Terrorism is likely to be a part of our world for as long as there is conflict about culture, race, politics and beliefs about how we should think and behave. But this does not mean that we cannot take action to minimise its impact, or change the circumstances that in the past have encouraged terrorists. The UN believes that sorting out other problems in the world, such as poverty, war, lack of education and injustice, may help to reduce the climate of hatred and fear in which terrorists are made.

Glossary

al-Qaeda the name often given to Islamic terrorists

Anarchist a person who promotes disorder or excites revolt against established rule

Anti-Semitism hatred of Jews

Assassination targeted murder of an individual

Biometrics physical identifiers such as fingerprints, iris patterns or genetic material

Civil war war between different groups within a single country

Coalition two or more countries united over a particular course of action

Counter-terrorism measures designed to defeat the terrorists

European Union (EU) a federation of European states

Fenians Irish nineteenth-century nationalists

Fundamentalists people with extreme religious views; sometimes called 'fanatics'

Ideology belief in a political idea such as democracy or communism

Imperial the rule or authority of a sovereign state over its dependencies

Insurgency a growing wave of rebellion

Jihadis the name sometimes given to those who believe they are fighting an Islamic 'holy war' against all things un-Islamic

Militant a person engaged in warfare or combat.

Occupation when an army from one country invades another and remains in charge

Oppressive not allowing free expression of views or behaviour

Paramilitaries fighters outside the regular armed forces who nevertheless have an army-type structure and leadership

Propaganda information, ideas, or rumours deliberately spread widely to help or harm a person, group, movement, institution, nation, etc

Regime the people in power; not necessarily freely elected

Sanctions measures (often economic) taken by one government against another in order to show strong disapproval and bring about change

United Nations (UN) an organisation of countries from all around the world that aims to promote peace, development and human rights

Weapons of mass destruction (WMDs) biological, chemical or nuclear weapons designed to inflict mass casualties on a civilian population

Weblinks

The United Nations
These two UN sites have useful information on terrorism and its causes:

The UN Action Against Terrorism
Updates on new measures and reports on what UN commissioners are doing to combat terrorism.
www.un.org/terrorism

Question of Palestine
A UN website reviewing the history and current status of the Arab/Israeli conflict.
www.un.org/depts/dpa/qpal

Conflict Archive on the InterNet
An academic resource with detailed information on the conflict in Northern Ireland, and accessible data on casualties.
www.cain.ulst.ac.uk

Electronic Frontiers Foundation
A US-based civil rights site, with thought-provoking articles on the many ways counter-terrorism can undermine liberty. Put terrorism in their Index Search to find related articles.
www.eff.org

The International Institute for Strategic Studies (IISS)
A London-based think-tank specialising in international security issues. They have published a paper examining trends in terrorism.
www.iiss.org

Israel/Palestine Center for Research and Information (IPCRI)
A joint Palestinian-Israeli think tank created to find solutions to the Arab/Israeli conflict. See especially their schools 'peace education' project.
www.ipcri.org/index1.html

The Terrorism Research Center
A terrorism consultancy bringing together research and expertise from several countries, including the UK, USA, France and Australia. Has some archive material and a very useful links page.
www.terrorism.com

Government SITES
The Northern Ireland Office
Slow, but well-connected government pages on Northern Ireland.
www.nio.gov.uk

The US Counter-terrorism Office
The official US government site for terrorism reports. The annual report identifies trends and lists organisations.
www.state.gov/s/ct

Note to parents and teachers:
Every effort has been made by the Publishers to ensure that these websites are suitable for children, that they are of the highest educational value, and that they contain no inappropriate or offensive material. However, because of the nature of the Internet, it is impossible to guarantee that the contents of these sites will not be altered. We strongly advise that Internet access is supervised by a responsible adult.

Index